An Original U-DRAW Book

Engelmann
the Footloose Christmas Spruce

Non-Illustrated Picture Book

Story by Lynn Mills
Illustrations by _____
(your name here)

First Edition

Copyright © 2016 Lynn Mills

All rights reserved, including the right to use or reproduce this book or portions thereof in any form whatsoever without written permission from the publisher except in the case of brief quotations embodied in critical articles or reviews.

Cosworth Publishing
21545 Yucatan Avenue
Woodland Hills CA 91364
www.cosworthpublishing.com

For information regarding permission,
please send an email to office@cosworthpublishing.com.

*Dedicated to Georgia and Veronica.
And Merry Christmas to all!*

Greetings to all Artists – and others.

Maybe you like to draw and color or maybe you don't.

Either way, these pages are easy.

Do them however you want to. Or don't do them at all.

Use any colors you want. Make a mess! Have some fun.

This is your book, so the art is all yours.

When you're finished, sign it with pride.

Engelmann and friends.

This is a good place to draw anything you want. Maybe a picture of yourself.

This one is easy. Draw a Christmas tree growing in the forest.

A forlorn young spruce stood six feet tall,
With feathery branches of green, but that's not all.
For he was the only one among the treelings
That had what you might call... feelings.
Was it just evergreen evolution?
Or the start of botanical revolution?

Show a Christmas tree at a Christmas tree lot. Add shoppers if you like.

Now waiting patiently on the Christmas tree lot
He watched with sadness as his mates got bought.
Customers looked him up and down, and they all
Said, "Too short!" "Too tall!" "Too big!" "Too small!"

This is your chance to draw pink Christmas trees. Why not?

And as Christmastime neared, he often feared
That he'd end up spending the holiday among the weird
Pink flocked trees no one wanted year after year,
And he asked himself, "What am I doing here?"

Show a family taking a special Christmas tree home.

His question was answered by a family named Hurley
Which numbered five, all dark haired and curly.
They loaded him up and when they got him home,
Placed him in the den where he was never alone,

This is where the family decorates the tree – and so can you. Make it the most beautiful tree you've ever seen, with all your favorite decorations.

    Dressed with antique treasures of hand-blown glass,
    Which hung beside trimmings the kids made in class,
    With a pipe cleaner star. And it must be mentioned
    He certainly loved being the center of attention.
    The family said, "It's our best Christmas tree ever!"
    "Have we had a better one?" "No, no, never."
    They played festive songs, and sang in harmony,
    That old classic carol, "O Christmas Tree!"

Here the family sees how special the tree is and they name him Engelmann.

The kids strung popcorn (though they ate nearly a mile)
But as they draped it... it seemed to smile,
Under two shiny balls – "Wait, did one of them wink?"
Asked one of the kids. "You know, what I think?
This isn't an ordinary tree. We have to give him a name."
So they thought and they thought, but nothing came,
Till one read his species name on his tag. "Let me introduce,
The one! The only! Engelmann, the Spruce!"

The family gathers around Engelmann to make and wrap Christmas gifts.

Each day they watered him to keep him fresh
And lay under his boughs to rearrange the crèche.
Spent nights camped at his foot, under a sheet
Watching holiday films like "Miracle on 34th Street."
They gathered beneath Engelmann to craft homemade gifts,
Gluing and knitting and wrapping in shifts.

Show the children studying the gifts and wondering...

Each night they laid gifts 'neath his aromatic boughs,
"Here's another one, Engelmann. Why, look at you now!"
As each box was positioned, his lights blinked with pride
While the children just wondered what must be inside.

Did the tree move? Maybe. It definitely rang its bells. Show the children's surprise.

"What do you think, Engelmann?" of a box made of shells,
And the tree answered... by ringing its bells.
The children's eyes widened, "I think he approves."
"Who would believe it? But I just saw him move."

What do you think Engelmann looks like in the dark with his lights glowing?

On Christmas Eve, Mom read the kids' favorite stories,
Reciting "*Night Before Christmas,*" like repertory.
They switched off the lights, all except for Engelmann, the Spruce,
Turning the walls golds and reds, silvers and blues.

Draw the kids saying, "Good night," to Engelmann before they go to bed.

His reflection resembled a thick forest on the ceiling
Creating an enchanted, magical feeling.
The kids went to bed without any fight,
And told Engelmann, "Thank you, good tree. And good night."

Show the excitement of Christmas morning around the tree.

Then the next morning, being Christmas Day,
The eager young children could finally play

How about drawing a picture of the kids with all their Christmas presents?

With all the toys Santa Claus had just brought them
And the other goodies their parents had bought them.
The Hurleys took photos in front of the tree
And Engelmann felt he was part of the family.

A Christmas wreath is easy to draw. It's not so easy to make him talk.

He was happy until an artificial wreath,
(I think he said his name was Heath),
Said, "Enjoy it now. Christmas season is brief."
Engelmann simply stared at him in disbelief,

For the first time, Engelmann isn't so happy. How would he look different?

For he didn't know the typical plan,
That he'd soon be lying naked by the garbage can.
Poor Engelmann, being perceptive, it would surely disturb
To know that he'd soon be out on the curb.

Draw the kids going back to school and leaving Engelmann behind.

By New Year's Eve, he'd lost a few needles,
But the Hurleys listened to their children's wheedles
And kept Engelmann up in all his glory.
But alas, that's not the end of the story.
For one day, it was no longer the season of Yule
So, sadly, the kids had to go back to school.

Show Mrs. Hurley taking down all of Engelmann's decorations.

And Mrs. Hurley thought it no longer cool
To vacuum pine needles, so she got boxes and stool
And without giving Engelmann the chance to dissent
She stripped off his lights and each ornament.
The kids said, "No, no! Mama, the tree is our friend!"
But she said, "Sorry, my dears. All good things must end."

Oh, no. Engelmann's out on the street alone. What would that look like?

Engelmann joined the ex-Xmas trees, growing brown in the heat,
Lying forgotten out there on the street.
With just a few remaining stray lines of tinsel,
Their wood no good for even a pencil.
Engelmann had felt like he was the Christmas host
And it distressed him to know that he'd soon be compost.

Show the kids walking past Engelmann on their way to the school bus.

    The kids sadly said, "'Bye" as they walked to the bus stop.
    Their mother said, "This is an attitude that you must drop.
    Is all this truly necessary?
    We go through it every January.
    I don't suppose you all remember
    That we'll get another tree come next December?"

The school bus is leaving. Make the children look sad.

And the kids said, "No, this year it's different.
We think Engelmann might be... intelligent."

Their mother said, "Go to school! The tree leaves today."
They knew she meant business, and went on their way.

Show the recycling truck coming. And Engelmann is afraid.

So Engelmann stood on the street, stripped and humbled
And soon, he heard - and felt - a low rumble
Growing strong as the voracious recycling truck loomed.
When he saw what it did, Engelmann knew he was doomed,
As mechanized arms plucked the tree across the street,
And threw it into the back, where it was chopped into peat.

Somehow Engelmann runs away. Mrs. Hurley chases him.

> That was a fate that Engelmann did refuse
> And somehow or other managed to infuse
> The power of movement in his cross-wood base,
> And so Mrs. Hurley had to give chase.

Even a policeman can't catch Engelmann. Draw the chase.

Engelmann dashed down the street at such a great speed
A cop thought he was a big, green tumbleweed.
Mrs. Hurley cried, "Oh please, stop my Christmas tree!"
And Engelmann thought, "Forget it, lady, you can't catch me!"

The kids on the school bus see Engelmann being chased. How would you react if you saw a Christmas tree that could run?

> He ran past the school bus stopped at the light
> And all the kids cheered the remarkable sight.
> The Hurley kids shouted, "Run, Engelmann! ...Run?"
> (There was never a ride to school quite this much fun.)
> As the bus stopped for some new kids climbing aboard
> The Hurleys leaped out the back, but they were ignored.

What would this crazy chase look like? Draw all the action.

They ran to catch Engelmann, raced in his direction,
Ducked behind parked cars, to avoid Mom's detection.
The Hurley kids' sneakers slipped, squished and sloshed
When they had to chase Engelmann through the local car wash.
They all ran through the mall but had to bail
When folks tried to buy Engelmann in an after-Christmas sale.
A plucky brown puppy lunged and barked
As Engelmann and the kids ran past, through the park.

Show the kids making a plan with Engelmann near some trees in the park.

The Hurleys cornered Engelmann near a thick grove of pines
And brainstormed a plan like little Einsteins.
"Engelmann," they urged him, "Instead of causing a riot
If you stand still, right here, maybe she'll buy it."

Draw the kids hiding behind Engelmann while crows gather around.

So Engelmann stopped to blend in and then froze,
To look part of the grove, as crows perched on his nose.
Mrs. Hurley had left on a few scattered things
And hungry, the birds pecked at his popcorn strings.
They picked off his tinsel to use for their nests
While the kids tried to shoo them off, the big pests.
The kids hid behind Engelmann as their mother approached.
They knew if she found them they'd be soundly reproached.

Draw the birds tickling Engelmann until Mrs. Hurley spots him.

As Mrs. Hurley came close, Engelmann couldn't stay in his pose,
For the great big birds tickling him did expose
That this was their own Engelmann the Spruce,
And his stint as a park tree was simply a ruse.
As he hopped and shook to pry the birds loose
Mrs. Hurley spied him – and the kids - but opted for a truce.

Mrs. Hurley makes a deal with Engelmann and the children.

To the kids, "I'll drive you to school, but won't fake any passes,
You'll take the heat from your teachers in all of your classes."
To Engelmann, "Dear tree, despite your agility, you're still my responsibility."
And as, deep down, all trees desire stability,
When Mrs. Hurley said, "Let's figure this out,"
Engelmann gave up and went back to the house.

Draw the kids coming home and finding that Engelmann is still there, waiting for them!

So the kids left for school and Engelmann stood still in the yard,
Waiting and waiting... the waiting was hard.
But when the children came home,
And saw him next to the gnome,
They sprang towards him, hugged him and cheered,
Which made something happen that's really quite weird.

Picture Engelmann growing roots into the ground in front of the house.

At the end of his trunk, Engelmann sprouted shoots
Which dug into the ground... becoming roots!
Then the life's blood of a tree – the sap - started flowing,
And everyone knew that Engelmann would be going
Nowhere. Mom even said she rather liked Engelmann's spot.
"He'll shield the house well when the weather turns hot."

Picture a happy Engelmann living in the front yard, and the kids playing around him.

So now the children enjoy Engelmann all through the year
And he's happy too, the one-time mutineer.
There are peaceful picnics under his shade,
As well as many a wild escapade.
For all Engelmann wanted was to be loved always,
Not just for the brief Christmas holidays.
And now that the cones sprung on Engelmann's branches
Have sprouted, the Hurleys have Christmas tree ranches.
So when you pick out your tree come next Christmas season
If it gets footloose, for whatever the reason,

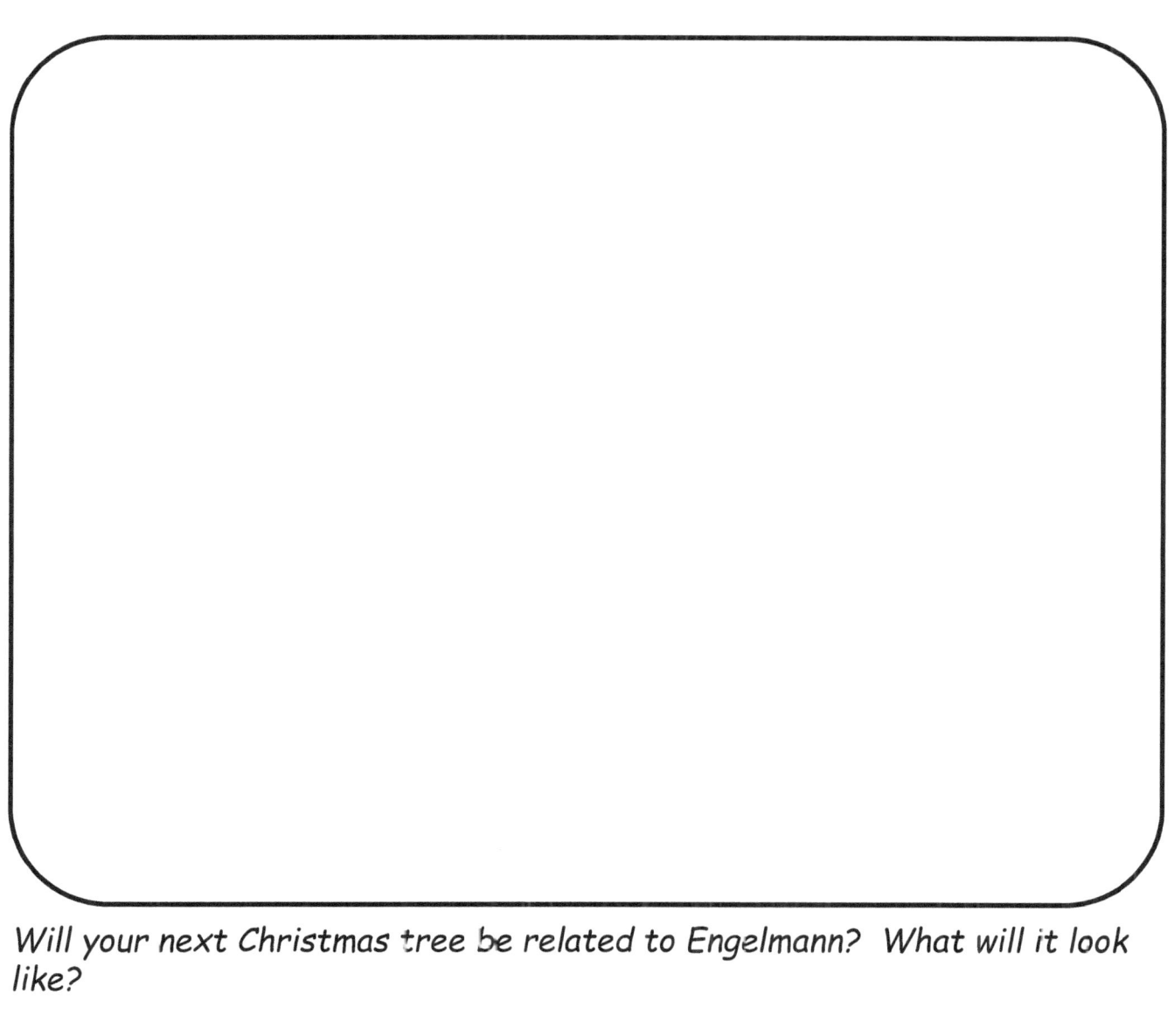

Will your next Christmas tree be related to Engelmann? What will it look like?

Now you know the truth, and can safely deduce
It's not just any tree... it's a descendent of Engelmann, the Spruce.

THE END

Engelmann the Footloose Christmas Spruce is author Lynn Mills' first children's book.

Lynn lives in Southern California, and loves reading Christmas books to her daughters every Christmas Eve... even though they are now in their 20s.

lm@bylynnmills.com

You might also like our other U-Draw Books.
(www.u-drawbooks.com).

Check out
Nate-Nate the Christmas Snake Non-Illustrated Picture Book
and also take a look at
The Magic of Fairy Falls Non-Illustrated Picture Book.
(written by a fifth grader, especially for kids.)

U-Draw books from Cosworth Publishing offer kids a chance to add their own creatve artwork to illustrate these books.
www.u-drawbooks.com

The Magic of Fairy Falls
Engelmann the Footloose Christmas Spruce
Nate-Nate the Christmas Snake
Why Can't Mommy Spend More Time with Me?
Rat BLEEP and Alien Poop

Other books from Cosworth Publishing
www.cosworthpublishing.com

The I Hate to Read Book
...and I Hate Math 2: Who Needs It?
Nate-Nate the Christmas Snake
The Dyslexic Handbook: Genius Edition
The OCD Funbook: Really?
The Attention Deficit Disorder Hyperactive Cookbook: Puzzle Edition
The Big Beautiful Book of Burping, Belching & Barfing
Cussing for Kids!: Etiquette for the Profane
The Bedtime Book of Bad Dreams: Dozing Dangerously
Baby's First Instruction Manual: How To Be the Center of the Universe
Is This Your First Funeral? A Child's Primer
How to Write This Book
Autism for Beginners: Surfing the Spectrum
The First Apology Is the Worst
The Book Book: Inside the Inside Story
The Amazing, Stupendous, Extraordinary, and Somewhat Unusual Spinning Book
Don't Go to College, Go to Europe for Less
That Damn Little Angel
Why Can't Mommy Spend More Time with Me?
So You Really Want a Dog?
Engelmann the Footloose Christmas Spruce

Thanks for buying, borrowing, or swiping this wonderful book.

At Cosworth Publishing we truly appreciate that, and in return, we'd like to offer you one of our E-books absolutely free—and worth every penny.

Just let us know that you want it, and we'll make sure that you get it. Let us know which book you read so we don't send you the same one.

Send an email to *office@cosworthpublishing.com*.

Then, from time to time, we will let you know via email when we have a new book that you might be interested in.

We won't do that very often because we're basically pretty lazy, and we don't produce very many new books.

www.ingramcontent.com/pod-product-compliance
Lightning Source LLC
Chambersburg PA
CBHW082041080526
44578CB00009B/795